"He who wants to persuade should put his trust not in the right argument, but in the right word."

—Joseph Conrad, Polish-born British novelist

Persuasive Proposals and Presentations

24 Lessons for Writing Winners

HEATHER PIERCE

McGraw-Hill

New York Chicago San Francisco Lisbon
London Madrid Mexico City Milan New Delhi
San Juan Seoul Singapore Sydney Toronto

The **McGraw·Hill** Companies

5 6 7 8 9 0   DOC/DOC   0 9 8 7 6

ISBN: 0-07-145089-0

McGraw-Hill books are available at special quantity discounts to use as premiums and sales promotions, or for use in corporate training programs. For more information, please write to the Director of Special Sales, Professional Publishing, McGraw-Hill, Two Penn Plaza, New York, NY 10121-2298. Or contact your local bookstore.

 This book is printed on recycled, acid-free paper containing a minimum of 50% recycled de-inked fiber.

To order
*Persuasive Proposals
and Presentations*
call 1-800-842-3075

Contents

☑ *Introduction*

Proposals and presentations can make or break a deal. Often they're the first (and sometimes only) tangible representation of your experience and qualifications. Winning proposals and presentations embody a successful sales strategy that shows an understanding of the client's needs and an ability to exceed their expectations when given the opportunity. Some contracts are awarded on the strength of the proposal alone.

Proposals that fail to win the deal often lack a consistent theme and don't demonstrate a clear differentiation between the vendor and its competition. They aren't persuasive in conveying qualities that convince the client of the vendor's superiority, and they're usually written more from the vendor's perspective than the client's.

A poorly written proposal or presentation makes you appear to be unorganized, disinterested, and unqualified. Clients will assume they can expect more of the same if they award you the business. A well-written proposal or presentation vaults you to the next step in the buying process and solidifies your client's confidence in a successful future partnership.

Whether you're presenting to your client for the first time, responding to a formal Request for Proposal (RFP), or submitting an informal proposal on your own initiative, it's worthwhile to make sure that every proposal and presentation represents your absolute best work.

For clients, the process of choosing a vendor often involves deciding between several companies with similar qualifications. They all appear to have the ability to satisfy the client's needs and deliver an acceptable product or service. Your proposal or presentation can either portray you as equal to the competition or elevate your status above the others. When a client is faced with a decision between "acceptable" and "exceptional," which do you think he or she will choose?

Proposals and presentations that are truly exceptional start with a winning strategy. Understand your audience and speak directly to them to build rapport and facilitate a partnership. Establish a theme for your proposal to convey key points. Decipher your clients' hidden messages and anticipate exactly the right way to showcase your strengths. Take every opportunity to highlight your experience and qualifications in the context of how it benefits the client.

Be persuasive, but stick to the point with content that's clear, concise, and organized. Validate your commitment to quality by giving your clients a document that's amazingly easy to read and grammatically flawless. Follow directions as if the deal depends on it—and often it does!

With these lessons as your guide, your proposals and presentations will play a major role in a successful sales strategy and you'll have all the elements you need to write winners.

"Of the modes of persuasion furnished by the spoken word there are three kinds. The first kind depends on the personal character of the speaker; the second on putting the audience into a certain frame of mind; the third on the proof, provided by the words of the speech itself."

—*Aristotle*

PART 1: Develop a winning strategy

☑ *Get agreement up front*

*L*ike good politicians, we're taught to avoid controversy, especially in the workplace. While this strategy may work well for winning elections, it's definitely not the best way to write winning proposals.

Sometimes we meet with clients, listen carefully, take copious notes, and yet still have questions that arise later. It's especially important, when drafting a proposal or presentation, that you have all the answers, or almost all the answers, up front. Otherwise, you could violate the most basic proposal rule and give clients something that isn't what they want.

With a Request for Proposal (RFP), it's even more important to address issues as soon as possible. Don't gloss over things and assume your clients will see your side of it in the proposal. Immediately clear up questions and address areas where you may not meet clients' requirements *before* you spend hours on a proposal that won't be considered.

Clarifying the following issues will help you create a proposal that offers no unpleasant surprises and gives the client what they want:

RFP questions that you don't understand. Read the RFP thoroughly and make a list of outstanding questions. Set aside time with your clients to go through your questions and get agreement on what they're asking and what they're looking for in response. As a nice reward for being proactive, the things you learn will often help make your proposal stand out from the competition.

Requirements that you may not be able to accommodate. Suppose an RFP states that you must be in compliance with a certain government regulation in order to be considered. Perhaps your company isn't required to have compliance or is scheduled to be in compliance at a future date. Some things are deal breakers; find out right away if such issues take you out of contention.

After you've clarified exactly what your clients are looking for, you may realize they're requesting something that may not be your strong point. Don't panic—demonstrate your confidence and dedication to your client by presenting them with an alternative solution that's equivalent or better than what they requested.

Address issues early on: Before you begin writing, make sure you have all the information you need to create a proposal and presentation that gives your clients what they want.

Don't be shy . . . clarify: Talk to your clients about any questions you have and gain valuable information in the process.

Don't come unglued if there's something you can't do: Try to present alternative solutions that shed your products and services in a positive light and hopefully give your clients an even more desirable option.

"Do we have to talk in order to agree or agree in order to talk?"

—José Bergamín, Spanish writer

☑ *Involve the experts*

"*T*wo heads are better than one," as the saying goes. This is certainly true when proposals and presentations are being created. Improve the quality of your content and make sure it's accurate and up to date by consulting the subject matter experts in your organization.

Involve experts in the strategy and execution of your proposal or presentation. Give them questions that are highly technical or otherwise beyond your area of expertise. You'll be glad you left the tough questions to the experts, and your content will be better for it.

Here are some examples of how experts can contribute to the success of your bid:

Prior to creating your proposal or presentation. Assemble a team from relevant areas in your organization to form a strategy for exactly what you're going to present to the client. Involve someone who can speak directly about the virtues of your product or service. Have him or her analyze the client's needs and determine the best solution for you to propose.

Example: You've received a Request for Proposal (RFP) from a company looking to replace its outdated sorting machine. You ask your head engineer to do a comparison of your machines with what the client currently has and what the competition is offering. He determines that your new RJ4 machine will save the client $1.2 million a year over their current machine and more than $450,000 over the competition. Now you have something specific to talk about in your proposal that could make the difference in winning the sale.

During the writing process. Rather than trying to address each and every issue on your own, identify those that would be better answered by the experts on your team. Information you receive from those closest to the subject matter will typically be more accurate, detailed, and timely than what you write from scratch or try to pull from old sources.

Example: A client who is seeking supply chain consulting services wants case studies of similar projects on which you've worked. You could pull the old standbys, or you could have your supply chain project manager read the RFP and come up with some examples based on her recent experiences in the field. Once she knows what the client is looking for, chances are she'll be able to draft a response that is more timely and specific to the client's needs.

When you receive information from your experts, it's important to incorporate it seamlessly into your proposal or presentation. Take technical, detailed information and make it easily understandable. Edit the content to ensure that it's consistent with the rest of the proposal and, above all, make sure it relates directly to the needs of your audience.

Don't work alone: Involve a team of experts who will help you propose the best solution for the client.

Delegate to make it great: For content that's accurate, detailed, and timely, ask the experts for assistance in drafting the proposal or presentation.

Pull it all together: Integrate responses from your experts to ensure consistency, comprehension, and focus on client needs.

"If you wish to succeed, consult three people first."

—Chinese proverb

☐ Interpret everything
literally

☑ *Read between the lines*

Successful sales efforts almost always involve an element of intuition. Most clients prefer to be somewhat mysterious in order to receive proposals that are "genuine"; they judge from those which vendor is the best at understanding and fulfilling exactly what they need. To determine the needs of clients who are often guarded about their motives, you need the ability to read between the lines to create an effective strategy for winning the deal.

Clients typically write questions to elicit a certain response or obtain specific information from you. It gives them the opportunity to compare responses and determine which vendor is the best qualified. It's to your advantage to avoid taking each question literally. Figure out what the client is truly getting at and, in addition to answering the question, expand upon the features and benefits of what you can provide them.

Here are some standard questions and the hidden messages behind them:

Question: "What percentage of your customers do you retain every year?"

Hidden Message: "Do you treat your customers well enough to keep them coming back for more?"

Question: "Will you guarantee not to increase rates for a period of two years?"

Hidden Message: "If we choose you as a vendor, can we trust you not to immediately jack up your prices?"

Question: "Do you have any additional suggestions beyond what is requested in this proposal?"

Hidden Message: "Can you 'think outside the box' to present unique, creative, and strategic solutions that set you apart from your competition and save us time and money?"

As the creator of the proposal or presentation, you will always find it beneficial to be privy to the strategy behind how your organization will be selling to the client. Putting yourself in the mindset of your clients will make interpreting the hidden messages easier and help you zero in on issues that will win the deal.

Use lessons from Psychology 101: Successful sales efforts often require that you read between the lines to determine a strategy that satisfies clients' needs that aren't explicitly stated.

Look for hidden messages: A question isn't just a question. It's also a subtle way for clients to obtain specific, revealing information from you.

Understand the strategy: An awareness of your organization's sales strategy helps put you in the mindset of the client to create a proposal or presentation that's effective in addressing their needs.

"The only real valuable thing is intuition."

—Albert Einstein

☐ Assume audiences are the same

☑ *Write for your audience*

*Y*ou wouldn't give the same birthday present to every family member, so why give all of your clients the same proposal or presentation? Each audience is unique, and they usually want to be treated that way.

Clients want to know that you're speaking directly to them, with an understanding of their specific needs and concerns. More importantly, they want to know that what you're offering is exactly what they're seeking.

It's helpful to write not only for the company to which you're selling but also to the individual decision maker. Is the decision maker highly analytical and persuaded mainly by facts and data, or does he or she make decisions based on a gut feeling or amicable relationship with the salesperson? Cover all the bases, but focus your efforts in areas that are most influential in winning the deal.

Before you can write for your audience, you have to *know* your audience. Do your homework. Learn about their organization and how they conduct business. And, above all, understand why they're coming to you with a problem to solve and how you plan to solve it.

Here are some ways to know your customers better:

Talk to them! Ask them about what they do and how their organization operates. Like most people, clients are usually happy to talk about themselves, their careers, and their companies. You'll learn a lot from these conversations and you'll help create the rapport you need throughout the sales process.

Feel their "pain." Once you know why your clients are coming to you for help, you'll be better equipped to offer solutions that solve their problems. Take a tour of their factory or talk to other vendors to get the big picture, beyond just what is written in the Request for Proposal (RFP). Often the key to knowing what they need is to find out what they're not saying.

Research, research, research. With the volume of information available on the Internet, there's no excuse for not at least visiting your client's Web site, printing a few screens, and jotting down some notes. Google.com and Hoovers.com are two popular online resources for company information.

Write for a specific audience: Understand that every client is unique, and tailor your content accordingly.

Know your client: Learn as much as you can about your client and the organization before you begin creating your proposal or presentation.

Do your research: Read the RFP, use the Internet, and ask questions to learn as much as you can about your audience.

"An audience is never wrong."

—Billy Wilder, U.S. film director

☑ *Focus on a theme*

*T*heme songs are usually associated with successful products. For a successful proposal that's music to your clients' ears, make sure you've got a theme they want to hear.

Identifying the top one or two reasons why your client is requesting your products and services will help you determine the theme of your proposal. Is the client trying to cut costs and achieve greater efficiency? Does the client need to be more competitive? Is there a requirement to which the client must comply? Once you know the one thing each client really wants to hear from you, then stick to that theme and support it throughout the proposal.

Here are some examples:

The client is looking for a product that increases efficiency and saves money. Luckily, you have just such a product to meet that client's needs. Your theme is something like "our product will make your operation run twice as fast at half the cost." Be specific, and substantiate your theme at every opportunity.

Your consulting firm has unique experience the client needs to help them become more competitive. You happen to have the best-qualified people who will do a great job for the client. Your theme is "you came to the right place. Our firm is the best choice because of the relevant experience of our consultants and our history of proven success." Once again, make sure your theme is specific, and support it with information relevant to your audience.

The government is requiring that your client obtain the liability insurance you provide by the end of the year. Even though clients are coming to you because they have to, not because they necessarily want to, it's still a good opportunity for you to find a theme that differentiates you from the competition. Show your client you have the product to keep them in compliance and also explain its additional benefits. Your theme is, "Yes, we have want you need, and we also have what you didn't even know you needed."

Clients often raise a variety of concerns when they look for a vendor or issue a Request for Proposal (RFP). With your theme in mind, address these issues and find a way to tie your responses back to the theme. By developing, emphasizing, and supporting your theme, you'll soon have your clients humming along, too.

Sing your theme song: Determine the one thing your clients want to hear from you and make that your theme throughout your proposal or presentation.

Be specific: Hone your theme so that it's directly relevant to the client's needs, and substantiate any claims you make.

Support your message: Take the individual issues that the client presents and address them with your theme in mind.

"To produce a mighty book, you must choose a mighty theme."

—Herman Melville

☑ Use their questions to frame your benefits

*T*he point when you answer your clients' questions isn't the time for "just the facts." Your responses give you the opportunity to convey that not only are you able to do exactly what they ask, but you also have unique strengths and qualifications that set you apart from the competition. Using clients' questions to frame your benefits throughout the proposal allows you to consistently highlight what makes your organization special.

Answer their questions completely, but leave room for expanding on your strengths and downplaying potential weaknesses. Respond directly, yet show your clients you understand what they're looking for and can deliver a product or service that is second to none.

These examples show the difference between "just the facts" and "justification" for why you're unique among the competition:

Question: "What percentage of your customers do you retain every year?"

Just the facts: "We retain an average of 98 percent of our customers every year."

Justification: "Our customer retention rate is among the highest in our industry, at 98 percent, and our dedication to our customers has been recognized by the J. D. Powers & Associates Award for Outstanding Customer Service."

Question: "Do all your products meet applicable safety standards?"

Just the facts: "Yes, our entire product line meets the applicable standards for safety."

Justification: "Yes, our products are in absolute compliance with all applicable standards for safety. The two products that offer the best solution for your needs are considered the safest in the industry, according to hazard reports from more than 10,000 users over a five-year period."

Question: "Will you guarantee not to increase rates for a period of two years?"

Just the facts: "Yes, our rates are guaranteed for up to two years."

Justification: "We offer a two-year rate guarantee, with a history of prices that have remained the same for more than five years. Long-standing relationships with our suppliers grant us significant discounts, with the cost savings passed on to our customers in the form of consistently low prices."

Remember that clients usually have several qualified vendors vying for their business. They won't choose one that simply "meets their needs." They'll choose one that clearly demonstrates they're the superior choice.

Be opportunistic: Seize the opportunity to tout your strengths throughout the proposal by highlighting key selling points in your responses to their questions.

Go beyond "just the facts": Answer clients' questions directly, but also include information that demonstrates the unique benefits of choosing you as their vendor.

Exceed expectations: Responses that show you "exceed" rather than just "meet" your clients' needs go a long way toward establishing your organization as the clear winner.

"We are not permitted to choose the frame of our destiny. But what we put into it is ours."

—Dag Hammarskjöld, Swedish statesman

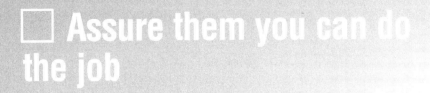

☐ Assure them you can do the job

☑ *Detail your qualifications*

*W*hen deciding with whom to spend their money, clients aren't likely to just "take your word for it." They want to see a detailed description of your experience and a list of qualifications. As you create your proposal or presentation, try to stay away from vague statements and include information that specifies what you bring to the table.

Clients want to be convinced that you are the best choice. You can tell them you're the best choice or you can *show* them you're the best choice. Think of your clients as "Doubting Thomases." They aren't inclined to believe your assurances unless you have the experience and qualifications to back them up.

Avoid the vague and make it convincing:

Vague: "We have completed similar projects with great success."

Convincing: "Our 10 years of proven success in supply chain management solutions can be seen in our work for ABC Company. The cost savings and efficiencies achieved at ABC are evidence of our experience and demonstrate how our expertise will also work for your organization."

Vague: "Customer service is at the core of our business."

Convincing: "For clients like ABC Company, we have demonstrated our dedication to customer service by offering money-back guarantees, next-day replacement of parts, and a 24-hour support department to solve any issues that may arise."

Vague: "We are financially stable."

Convincing: "Every year throughout our 12-year history, national banks and independent rating services certify that our financial stability is among the best in the industry. We're pleased to share this data along with a copy of our annual report."

For every piece of information you provide, explain to your clients why it's important. Or, more specifically, explain why it's important to them and how it will help you do a better job of providing them the product or service they're seeking. When you talk about the "how" of your business and explain "why" your clients should choose you, you'll be well on your way to writing a winning proposal.

Clients won't "take your word for it": Give them a detailed description of your experience and qualifications.

Don't tell, show: Make your case by showing clients how your expertise has benefited previous clients.

Be convincing, not vague: Vague assurances aren't as effective as specific examples and real evidence of your experience and qualifications.

"We judge ourselves by what we feel capable of doing, while others judge us by what we have already done."

—Henry Wadsworth Longfellow, U.S. poet

☐ Include the standard case studies

☑ *Draw on industry experience*

*T*hey say that "the proof is in the pudding." One of the ways to prove you have the talent and experience to be a successful vendor is by including case studies in your proposal or presentation. Case studies illustrate successful projects and act as real-life examples of your work. Clients are usually very interested in this information because it's their best glimpse of what you'll be like when you're working for them.

You should take the time to document your work and have a variety of case studies at your disposal. If reading that last sentence caused a pang in the pit of your stomach and a flutter in your heart, don't worry. Standard case studies aren't always the best information to present. You should talk about your industry experience relevant to each client to make a persuasive case for your expertise.

Here's how to prepare great stories to tell your clients:

Know what your client is looking for. Read the Request for Proposal (RFP) carefully, talk to your client, figure out the information that's going to persuade the client, and seal the deal.

Consult the experts in your organization. Talk to your colleagues who specialize in projects relevant to your client. Have them read the RFP and draft some examples of work they've done for similar customers.

Draw parallels. Illustrate examples of how your previous work mirrors exactly what the client wants you to do for them.

Example: "For our client at ABC Company, we created a unique solution that resulted in twice the manufacturing capacity and more than $250,000 in cost savings. A similar solution implemented at your organization will have comparable results, coupled with dramatic improvements in efficiency that our veteran consultants will help you facilitate."

Just as you would customize your personal résumé for the job to which you're applying, you want to be sure your case studies are written with the client in mind. Detail your experiences and talk about how your industry expertise makes you the best-qualified vendor for the job.

Use real-life examples: This is often the best way for clients to see how you'll work for them.

Tell a great story: Know the client's needs and use the experts in your organization to create relevant examples of your work.

Make the past the future: Draw parallels between your previous experience and the similar success you'll have working for your client.

---

*"Past experience, if not forgotten,
is a guide to the future."*

—*Chinese proverb*

☐ **Make bold claims**

☑ *Substantiate bold claims*

*H*ave you ever eaten at a restaurant that claimed to serve the "World's Greatest Hamburgers"? You probably left thinking either, "it was a good hamburger, but I wouldn't say it was the 'world's greatest,'" or, "what a disappointment; I've had better hamburgers in my backyard."

There's nothing wrong with making bold claims as long as you have the facts to substantiate them. If you really do have the "world's greatest" something or other, by all means, tell your clients about it and provide evidence to support your claim. But if you're all talk and no action, it's best to leave the puffery to the burger makers.

The best and most convincing way to substantiate bold claims is through impartial, third-party reinforcement. Are there outside agencies or media outlets that have ranked your organization on certain criteria? Have industry sources reviewed your products and given them high marks? Your clients are most likely going to be swayed by testimonials from organizations other than yours, so use a combination of outside and internal information to support your claims.

Here are some common claims and ways to give them credence:

Claim: "We are the largest independent reseller of widgets in the United States."

Reinforcements: Industry rankings listing overall sales; articles in the media that feature your status in the marketplace; press releases; company financials.

Claim: "Our machine is the fastest and most reliable in the industry."

Reinforcements: Independent product reviews and rankings; testimonials from satisfied customers; service records.

Claim: "Consultants at XYZ Company are the industry's top experts in organizational change."

Reinforcements: Published articles, either written by the consultants or about them, on topics related to the client's business; résumés; case studies; client testimonials.

Keep supporting documentation easily accessible, and always be on the lookout for positive mention of your company, product, or service in the general media and industry publications. This independent information helps add credibility to your experience and qualifications. And, if you're lucky enough to have bold claims to make, they will mean more to your audience when they're supported by a source other than yourself.

Prove it: Bold claims differentiate your organization from the competition, but they'll be met with skepticism from your client if they're not substantiated.

Bring in the outsiders: Supporting information from impartial, outside sources helps your clients see you're not the only one who thinks you're the greatest.

Be an information gatherer: Create a library of internal and external information you can use to make a convincing argument for your achievements and keep it current.

"Well done is better than well said."

—Benjamin Franklin

☑ *Use endorsements to make your case*

*O*ne of the most frustrating things in business, and in life, is our inability to predict the future. If we could, we'd all make millions on the stock market and your clients would know, without even glancing at the proposal or presentation, that your organization is clearly the best choice. In the absence of the crystal ball, as far as your clients are concerned, the past often dictates the future. They want to know you have a history of happy customers willing to talk about their positive experience with your company.

Endorsements and testimonials are a great way to show your client how they can be the next lucky benefactor of your excellent product or valuable service. Find customers in the same industry who have achieved results similar to what the client is seeking. Ask your best customers if they are familiar with your client, their organization, or both, and would be willing to provide a glowing endorsement.

There are several common ways for customers to endorse your product or service. Using a combination of these will help you both in the content of the proposal or presentation and in the client's final decision-making process.

Customer quotes: Use these to highlight your strengths and successes. It's usually most effective to have your customers write their own testimonials, though sometimes they may ask you to write them with their approval. Reinforcement from current customers adds a great deal of credibility to your sales pitch.

References: Most Requests for Proposal (RFPs) ask for references, so you should always be prepared for clients to speak directly with your top customers. But don't assume the same customers are always happy to talk to every Joe Prospect who comes calling. Check with your customers *before* you list them as a reference and give them some background about the client. The best reference is a well-informed, satisfied customer who won't be caught off guard.

Just as good references can seal the deal, bad references can be very harmful. Remember the old saying "if you can't say anything nice, don't say anything at all" when it comes to endorsements. If you're grasping for positive testimonials, it's best to find another way to support your strengths.

The past dictates the future: Your client's best glimpse of how you'll work for them often comes from taking a look at how you've worked for customers in the past.

Endorse, of course: Include testimonials and references in your proposal to support key strengths and successes.

Ask for permission, not forgiveness: Obtain permission from your customers before using their testimonials or including them as a reference, and make sure they're still your number one fans when they talk to your client.

"It may be big, bold and brilliantly effective, but it was painted with about the same degree of feeling with which new cars are painted in Detroit."

—James Rosenquist

☑ *Show them how they benefit*

A winning proposal is not about you, it's about the client. Instead of telling them what you do and how you do it, show them how they will benefit from your products or services. Your clients don't want to know what you can do; they want to know what you can do for them.

Learn about your client's business and determine the specific needs you fulfill. Demonstrate your understanding of the client's goals and objectives by using customized examples of problems you can solve. Offering more than a generic description of your products and services shows you have taken the time to tailor your proposal or presentation to address issues of greatest importance to the client. Here are some examples:

Generic: "We offer a sorting machine that leads the industry in units per minute, thereby lowering costs and time to market."

Client-Focused: "Our sorting machine is the fastest in the industry. It will double the output of widgets in your Singapore plant at nearly half of your current $50 million cost."

Generic: "Our consultants have extensive industry knowledge and demonstrate a thorough understanding of our clients' businesses."

Client-Focused: "Our supply chain experts have more than 20 years of retail industry experience. Using our unique knowledge of ABC Company and its suppliers, we will determine strategies to achieve your goal of greater manufacturing efficiency by Q4 2006."

Write the proposal or presentation from the client's point of view. Put yourself in the mindset of the client by asking yourself these questions:

- Is every feature or benefit described with regard to how it fulfills a specific client need?
- Does the proposal or presentation use terminology and language that mirrors the client's language and demonstrates depth of knowledge of their business?
- Do product and service descriptions directly address what the client is seeking, or is there extraneous information that doesn't support the client's decision?

Look for ways you can benefit your client that go beyond the obvious. For example, a client wants a proposal for a series of brochures. Your firm also has multimedia capabilities that would complement the brochure design and add visual impact to the client's upcoming trade show.

Take the opportunity to discuss how you can offer the client a packaged solution, describing the benefits of delivering a consistent message, and saving the time and expense of working with multiple vendors. Client-focused upselling is a great way to explore new business opportunities and demonstrate added value.

Winning proposals are more than a description of what you do: Talk about what you can do for your clients and why you are the superior choice.

Customize language to focus on client needs: Understand your client's business and make sure that every feature or benefit is related specifically to solving a problem or fulfilling a need.

Write from the client's point of view: Your proposal or presentation should be written and structured from the client's perspective, giving them information that is customized, persuasive, and relevant to their decision-making process.

"It is those who can spot opportunities who are truly exceptional."

—Chinese proverb

☑ *Stand out as uniquely qualified*

*R*emember those T-shirts that asked, "Why be normal?" That's what you should be asking yourself as you create your proposal or presentation. One of the main reasons clients give for choosing another vendor is that they can't find anything that differentiates your organization from the rest of the field. When you're competing for business, don't try to look like everyone else. Try to come across as uniquely different *and* better than your competition.

Figuring out what differentiates your organization often requires some soul searching. Take a look at your client and your competition. Just as individuals have different life experiences, your organization has unique experience you can share.

Maybe you have employees who have worked for the client company and can provide insights that will help your proposal. Perhaps your current customer list includes experience with many companies related to your client's business. Identify what makes your organization unique, with respect to each individual proposal or presentation, and tell your client about it—often.

For example:

Client wants: A company that is long-standing and financially stable.

Your competition says: "We've been in business for 25 years and have annual sales of more than $100 million."

You're unique because: You've been in business for more than 20 years and have a long list of happy customers in your client's field who have been with you for more than 15 years. Having achieved the industry's highest financial rating year after year, your business maintains consistent profitability, which is reinvested in the business to continue offering new and improved products and services to your customers.

Convincing, huh? Your clients will think so, too. Dig deep to find out what differentiates your organization from the competition, and make sure the facts are relevant and persuasive to your audience. There's no reason to be "normal" when you can come across as unique and better than your competition.

Differentiate yourself: Don't blend in with the crowd. Give your clients a reason to choose you over the competition.

Do some soul searching: Look at your client and your competition, then look at your organization. Determine what makes you unique and talk about it in your proposal or presentation.

Be convincing: Talk about your differences, and use persuasive content that is highly relevant to your audience.

"Everything perfect in its kind has to transcend its own kind, it must become something different and incomparable."

—Johann Wolfgang von Goethe

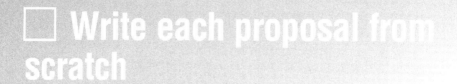

☐ **Write each proposal from scratch**

☑ *Pull the best from old winners*

*T*ime is usually of the essence when it comes to proposal writing, so why reinvent the wheel? The best approach is to start with a template that's formed from previous winning proposals.

Create an electronic library of information from which you can pull content to use in proposals and presentations. This capability proves especially beneficial for content that is relevant in nearly every proposal or Request for Proposal (RFP) response. Information such as the history of your organization, financial data, employee biographies, and case studies prove universally useful, provided you carefully choose information that relates directly to your audience.

Because you should tailor your proposal to address your client's unique needs and stick to a theme of greatest importance to them, it's crucial to keep your audience in mind when you are working with standard proposal content pulled from your library. Even if you've read it a thousand times, read your standard language again and find ways to customize it to make a persuasive argument for your client. Pulling the best from old winners doesn't necessarily mean it's the best for your current situation.

There may be occasions when it's justifiable to give your client a proposal that's primarily standard content. You may have a client just looking for general information on your organization, or a situation may occur in which a time crunch has you prioritizing a detailed RFP response for a major client over a prospect that doesn't represent the same revenue potential. Still, in every case, it's important to take the time to customize some part of the proposal, whether it's the cover letter, executive summary, or testimonials and references.

The biggest danger of pulling existing content for a new proposal is that you run the risk of sounding too generic or including information that isn't relevant to your client. And just about everyone has a horror story of sending out a proposal that actually had another client's name in it! The best way to avoid this and other proposal-writing mishaps is to read your proposal word for word before it goes out the door. By making sure it contains your best content, customized for your audience, you increase your chances of creating a proposal that ends up a winner.

Don't start from scratch: Use content from your winning proposals to create a library of information that will help you in creating new proposals and presentations.

Different proposals for different clients: The degree of standard content customization depends on the situation, but always personalize at least one aspect of your proposal.

Read it word for word: Use of existing content for a new proposal is wrought with pitfalls, unless you read the proposal carefully and make sure content that has worked in the past is going to win in the present.

"The only function that one experience can perform is to lead into another experience."

—William James, U.S. philosopher

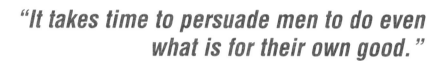

"It takes time to persuade men to do even what is for their own good."

—*Thomas Jefferson*

PART 2: Be clear, concise, and organized

✓ *Organize material exactly as they do*

*W*hat may seem perfectly logical to you may be, in the words of Mr. Spock, "illogical" to your audience. When you've taken the time to organize something in a certain way, you don't appreciate someone coming along and rearranging it. That's often how clients feel when they receive a proposal that doesn't follow their format. It's best to structure your response in the same order as the questions the client has provided.

In most Requests for Proposal (RFPs), you'll find the information arranged with the general questions up front (such as company history and overview), with the more detailed questions to follow. Pricing is almost always last. Government proposals often have highly specific requirements for how the proposal should be organized, and you should always follow their format.

When there is no specified format, you should organize your proposal according to some general guidelines. The following are some of the key components:

1. *A cover letter:* Important in almost every situation, a cover letter is especially so if the proposal is being sent to the client. Make it short, with just a couple of paragraphs of key points from your proposal.

2. *An executive summary:* The executive summary gives the client an overview of the entire proposal, usually in two pages or less. The executive summary is very important to the success of your effort, because it is sometimes the only thing the client will read. Make sure it's written with the client in mind and emphasizes information of greatest importance to them.
3. *The body of the proposal:* Most proposals start with company history and move on to descriptions of products and services, saving the benefits for last. It's a better idea to start with your key selling factors and save the extraneous information for the end of the proposal or the appendix.
4. *Pricing:* It's best to put the pricing at the end, even if some clients will look at it first. You want your clients to be sold on your organization before they have to worry about how much it will cost.

Even if you don't have a lot of control over how your information is organized, you do have control over how you present your information in each section or response. Just like a good reporter who states the key facts of a news story in the first paragraph, you should make sure your most persuasive arguments are stated up front.

Follow the leader: When your clients present information in a specific way, follow their lead and organize your response to mirror their structure.

Overview first, pricing last: When format is left up to you, it's best to include an executive summary up front and save the dollar signs for the end.

First things first: Emphasize critical selling points at the beginning of each section or response. Don't make clients wait to get to the heart of your sales pitch.

"In business you get what you want by giving other people what they want."

—Alice Foote MacDougall, U.S. businesswoman

☑ *Use plenty of heads and subheads*

*C*hances are your local newspaper has modified its format over the last few years. You've probably seen more headlines and subheads, sidebars, and captions. The primary reason for this is readability. We have grown impatient reading lengthy blocks of text and are tired of wading through a sea of black and white.

Learn from journalism experts and use plenty of headings and sub-headings when you create proposals and presentations. It gives clients a clear idea of the topic of your section and, like a Web site, allows them to easily identify information and skip to points of interest.

Using heads and subheads helps you highlight key points, and giving your headlines some pizzazz makes them memorable to your audience. You don't have to restate the obvious. Put some creativity into how you title your sections and outline your responses.

Here is an example of how good headlines and subheads enhance your proposal or presentation:

Stating the obvious:
Company history
 Historical timeline
 Number of employees
 Financial data

Getting creative:
A history of successful projects and satisfied clients
 38 years of service to your industry

Employees dedicated to customer service
Profits reinvested for continuous improvements

The same headlines and subheads can also apply to the titles and text of your presentation slides. Consider how you label forms and supporting information. Does every title reflect not just what it is but also why it's important to the client? Seize the opportunity to enhance the effectiveness of your key messages and the readability of your proposal or presentation format.

Be a headliner: Write for readability, and use heads and subheads to keep your clients from drowning in a sea of black and white.

Make it easy to find information: Like a Web site, headings and sub-headings call out important information and make it easy for your clients to locate.

Obvious is oblivious: Heads and subheads have more impact when you go beyond the literal and use them to highlight your key selling points.

"Don't agonize, organize."

—Florynce R. Kennedy

☑ *Address all subquestions individually*

*I*n proposals, it's important that you don't "just answer the question." You've got to answer the main question, and the subquestion below it, and the subquestion below that, and so on. Requests for Proposal (RFPs) are sometimes a veritable maze of questions. Just answering the first one in the series often leaves your client searching for more information and leaves you missing an opportunity to talk about your key selling points.

Don't just look at the heading of a section and paste in your standard content. Give every question and subquestion its own response. Avoid repeating yourself by including new information or putting a different spin on each question to which you're responding.

This gives you an idea of what to avoid:

Question: Describe the history of your company
    a. Corporate philosophy
    b. Employee statistics
    c. Financial stability

Insufficient Response: Our company was founded in 1971, and began as a partnership between the current president and chief financial officer. The successful evolution of our customer service–focused organization has brought us to where we are today, with 258 employees and more than $58 million in annual sales.

There are many missed opportunities in the above response, in addition to not fully answering the questions. It sounds like the client is curious about how you do business, not just your history. Did you tell them about how your corporate philosophy contributes to low turnover and high levels of customer satisfaction? Did you describe how you're one of the oldest and consistently profitable companies in your industry? Did you explain to your client how all of this makes you the best choice for his or her organization?

In the interest of time, it's easy to paste in a standard response to what appears to be a general question. But you'll do yourself and your client a favor by addressing each and every question or section of the RFP, remembering to use your responses to describe your product or service and how it benefits the client.

Don't just answer the question: Answer every question individually, no matter how general. Try to put a new spin on each response without too much repetition.

Avoid using standard content: By pasting in standard language that seems to answer the client's main question, you're probably leaving the client wanting more information.

Use every chance to sell yourself: Look at each response as an opportunity to promote your product or service to your clients and show them how they benefit.

"Every question we answer leads on to another question."

—Desmond Morris, British anthropologist

☐ Answer it once

☑ *Answer it each time it comes up*

Sometimes you'll receive a Request for Proposal (RFP) that resembles a patchwork quilt. It has sections that don't seem to match, with some parts that look identical. This often happens when the RFP is created by groups within an organization, with different people responsible for different sections. It usually means that these same people will be evaluating your proposal by reading only their sections.

It's important to write all of your proposals with the assumption that they won't be read from start to finish. If the same question seems to arise over and over, it's best to respond to it every time it comes up.

Here are some tips for making sure your content carries over from section to section:

Don't be afraid to repeat yourself: Your clients will appreciate that you've taken the time to fully answer their questions throughout the proposal, no matter how repetitious you think you're being. If your only response is "see here" or "refer to," you'll leave your clients hunting all over the proposal for information you could have easily included right there in your answer.

Don't overdo it: If you have a very lengthy response that you're asked to repeat over and over, include your entire response only the first time the question appears or in the most applicable place in the proposal. For repeat questions, include a summary rather than the entire answer and give your clients the option of referring to the complete response where you originally placed it.

Check the consistency: The repetition rule also applies to terminology, to avoid confusing your clients. Be consistent and use the same name for things throughout your proposal. For example, if you refer to your "Consulterrific" service, don't call it "Terrific Consulting" elsewhere in the proposal. It's okay to use abbreviations as long as you spell out the full name at the beginning of each section with the abbreviation in parentheses.

A client who is either confused by your content or has to work too hard to find answers is not going to feel good about the experience. Make a positive impression by submitting a proposal that's complete with all the information your client needs, even if you have to say it twice.

Proposal, interrupted: Clients often have different people review sections of the proposal, so it's best not to assume it will be read from start to finish.

Don't cheat, repeat: Don't leave your client searching for answers. Repeat your responses if your client repeats their questions.

Avoid a second term: Use consistent terminology throughout the proposal to avoid confusing your clients with multiple names and references to the same thing.

"It's the repetition of affirmations that leads to belief."

—Muhammad Ali

☐ **Insert résumés, drawings, charts, and so on**

☑ *Put it in the appendix*

Have you ever read an article online and come across a "learn more" button at the end? At that point, you're either satisfied that you've gleaned the main points of the article, or you're interested in finding more information on the subject. This should be the same concept used in your proposals. The main proposal should give your clients all the information they need, with the supporting documents in the appendix for clients who wish to "learn more."

Clients appreciate proposals that are concise and to the point; however, you never know when a client will be especially curious about a particular issue. It's best to write your proposal to include every key selling point you want to make and anticipate areas that may be of added interest by including relevant documents in the appendix.

Some common appendix items are:

- Charts, graphs, and spreadsheets
- Client lists and references
- News articles and press releases
- Employee résumés
- Case studies
- Annual reports

This is not to say that you shouldn't supplement your main proposal with graphic elements, bulleted lists, and summary data. These elements are important, but it's best to keep them as a modest complement to the text. If you've got a chart that takes up the entire page or full biographies of eight employees to include, you'll show consideration of your audience by summarizing the information in your main proposal and leaving the extended detail to the appendix.

Remember to reference appendix items in your main proposal text. For a question like, "What is your annual employee turnover?" you can answer it: "Annual turnover is 5 percent, which is extremely low for our industry and reflects our commitment to employee satisfaction. For more information, please see the appendix item titled, 'How XYZ Company Honors Its Employees,' an article about our company recently published in *BusinessWeek*."

Appendix items let clients "learn more": Get your key selling points across in the main proposal, but put supporting documents in the appendix for clients to retrieve additional information.

Move it to the back: Detailed documents and lengthy reports such as case studies and annual reports are valuable pieces of information that find a good home in the appendix.

Let clients know where to find it: Be sure to reference appendix items in your main proposal text so your audience can decide if they want more information and exactly where to look for it.

"The end crowneth the work."

—Elizabeth I, Queen of England

☐ Sound like an expert

☑ *Sound like a well-informed friend*

When it comes to writing proposals and presentations, remember that no one likes a know-it-all. While you definitely want your clients to know you're an expert in your field, you don't need to sound like one in your proposal. Your goal is to form a lasting partnership with the client, so it's a good idea to set a friendly tone right from the beginning.

An expert tells you how you should solve your problems. A well-informed friend helps you solve them. Clients need your information to make their decision, but let them be the experts while you act as the helpful ally eager to share your knowledge about your organization, products, and services and show how it will benefit them.

You can see the difference in the examples below:

Expert: Widgets made by XYZ Company are manufactured with titanium and are able to withstand dramatic temperature changes.

Friend: We make our fasteners out of titanium for increased durability and resistance to temperature extremes. Our product is designed to accommodate 24-hour use in your factories, even in the varying climates of your worldwide operations.

Expert: Supply chain efficiencies are best achieved by adopting a strategy pioneered by our organization.

Friend: Our consultants can help make your supply chain more efficient by partnering with your product experts to show them our unique strategy, which has proven successful for many other companies.

Showing your clients that you care about fulfilling their needs, not just telling them how great your product or service is, will make it easier for them to see you as a partner, not just a vendor. And you'll still achieve the goal of demonstrating to your clients that you have the expertise to provide them with a solution that satisfies their goals and objectives. After all, what are friends for?

Set a friendly tone: Portray yourself as an informed friend who can talk about your product or service in terms of how it benefits the client.

Talk with the client, not to them: Use language that is client-focused, with examples that demonstrate your knowledge and understanding of their goals and objectives.

Know it all, but don't be a know-it-all: Let the clients be the experts and you'll send a powerful message that facilitates true partnerships.

"Experience is not what happens to a man; it is what a man does with what happens to him."

—Aldous Huxley, British author

☑ *Stick to the point*

---

*B*elieve it or not, clients probably aren't too excited about reading your proposals. This is especially true if the documents are wordy enough to rival Tolstoy's *War and Peace.* Your goal is to inform and entice, not bore and exhaust. Make your proposal a joy to read (or at least not a chore) by sticking to the point.

We all know there are many ways to say the same thing. For proposals and presentations, your focus should be on writing as clearly and concisely as you can. Find the balance between making a persuasive argument and exhausting your subject. Make sure what you include is absolutely necessary, not just filler.

Here are some tips to make your proposals and presentations more readable:

Write like a journalist: Summarize the "who, what, when, where, why, and how" in the first paragraph and structure your responses with key points emphasized up front. Then provide a brief sentence or two of supporting information.

Use active, not passive voice: Think about how you write your résumé. Use the same persuasive language in your proposals and put the subject at the beginning of every sentence:

Passive: Many companies have been helped by our expertise.

Active: Our expertise helps many companies.

Keep your sentences and paragraphs brief: Without sounding choppy, try to limit the length of your sentences. If you're on the verge of a run-on, use your friend the period and start a new sentence. As a rule of thumb, limit paragraphs to no more than four or five sentences, to give your reader a visual break.

Sticking to the point with clear and concise content greatly increases the chance that your audience will read past the executive summary of your proposal. Not only does your client appreciate your brevity, but you will have less to write and you'll save a few trees when you print the final product.

Quick, clear and concise: Get to the point right away and include only the information that supports your initial statements.

Be active, not passive: Writing in active voice gets your point across more effectively and uses fewer words.

Avoid a run-on marathon: Enhance readability by keeping your sentences short and limiting your paragraphs to just a few sentences.

"Have common sense and . . . stick to the point."

—Somerset Maugham, famed storyteller

☑ *Get rid of jargon*

"*W*e need an ETA on those RFPs by COB." If you have no idea what that means, you're probably feeling the same way your clients do when they read a proposal filled with technical terms and jargon. When we do or say something frequently in our own workplace, we often forget that those outside our organization may not be familiar with our terminology. Give your clients the straight talk and avoid confusion by spelling out what you want to say.

While being careful not to talk down to your audience, make sure that the content of your proposal or presentation is carefully stated and fully understandable by the average reader. Chances are your audience consists of individuals with varying degrees of familiarity with your organization, so it's best to write content that everyone can understand.

Below are some ways to enhance the clarity of your proposal or presentation:

- *Refer to what your product is or does, rather than by its brand name:* If you offer the services of your top consultants in a package you have named "Consulterrific," make sure your client understands what the service entails, not just what you call it.
- *Find creative ways to explain technical concepts:* Use bullet points or step-by-step instructions to help your audience grasp detailed subject matter. Put yourself in their shoes and think about how you would want someone to explain it to you for the first time.
- *Conduct an impartial third-party review:* Have someone outside your organization review the proposal and give you feedback on its

readability. Is it clear what products and services you're proposing? This can be a great way for you to gauge the reaction of your audience.

Another way to speak your clients' language in proposals and presentations is to mirror the terminology they use. For example, if an insurance company refers to their field sales force as "distributors" instead of "agents," you'll demonstrate a good understanding of your client's corporate language by referring to "distributors" in your proposal. Sharing a common language is a great start to your future partnership.

Technically speaking, you shouldn't: Write your proposal or presentation content for the average reader, avoiding terms that are highly technical or used only in your organization.

Spell it out: Describe what your product or service does, not just its name, and find ways to illustrate difficult concepts as if you were seeing them for the first time.

Speak their language: Avoid your jargon, but include the client's in your proposal or presentation to demonstrate your understanding of the client's business.

"Jargon is part ceremonial robe, part false beard."

—Mason Cooley, U.S. aphorist

✓ Use lots of white space and wide margins

*I*s it just me, or are some business newspapers difficult to read? With tiny little type and very little space between columns, it makes them hard to get through. You have to be pretty serious about business to read them section by section. When it comes to reading your proposal, most clients also dread seeing pages filled with text.

Make your proposal more inviting by being generous with white space and wide margins. Don't assume that you're doing your clients a favor by giving them a proposal that includes all the information in a small number of pages. While brevity in your content is important, it's better to present a proposal with a lot of white space that's a little longer but much easier to read.

Here are some ways to create visual breaks and make your proposal a breeze to read:

- *Keep your paragraphs short:* Avoid creating huge blocks of text on the page by keeping your paragraphs to just a few sentences. Insert a space between paragraphs to create a visual break.
- *Use bullet points or numbering:* Both bullets and numbered lists are useful for highlighting information and making it easier to read than a paragraph format.
- *Use columns:* For long lists of information such as client lists or product names, split the information into two or three columns, with ample margins between them.
- *Align your text to the left:* Leave justified text for newspaper columns. For full-page business documents, it's better to avoid

the formality and odd spacing between words that happens when you fully justify text to both the left and right.

■ *Use a font size between 10 and 12 point for the body of your text:* Use larger sizes for headings and subheadings, but don't go overboard.

■ *Find appropriate uses for color:* Strategic use of color in headings or to highlight key points can contribute to the readability of your proposal. Stick to two or three different colors, use them consistently, and make sure that the document will also read well in black and white, if you or your client need to make black-and-white copies.

Leave a fairly wide margin around the top, bottom, and sides of your proposal. At the bottom, leave ample room between any footer information such as the document name, date, and page number, and the main text of your proposal. Your clients will appreciate that your formatting choices make their review process faster and easier.

Don't build a wall of text: Text-filled pages make reading your proposal seem like a daunting task; use white space and wide margins to enhance readability.

Create visual breaks: Break up the text by shortening your paragraphs, using bulleted lists, and having appropriate fonts and colors.

Increase your margins: Leave plenty of space around all edges of your page, especially on the sides and the bottom of the page between the footer and your main body text.

"Art consists of limitation. The most beautiful part of every picture is the frame."

—Gilbert Keith Chesterton, British author

☑ Insist on perfect grammar, spelling, and punctuation

*I*t's been said that if you dress shabbily, people notice the clothes. If you dress impeccably, they notice the person. The same philosophy also applies to the care you should take in proofreading your proposals and presentations. If they're wrought with bad punctuation and misspellings, your clients will have a hard time seeing past your lack of attention to detail. But if there are no errors to distract them, clients will focus on your message.

Build ample time into your schedule for proofreading the entire proposal or presentation before it goes to your client. Make proofreading a priority, not just something to do if you have time. Your proposal or presentation is, in effect, your first project for the client. You want it to mirror the quality, customer service, and attention to detail you're trying to sell them on. A less-than-perfect document may leave your clients wondering if your product or service will be less than perfect, too.

Here are some questions to ask as you edit your proposal or presentation:

- Are there errors in grammar, spelling, and punctuation?
- Do the responses fully answer the questions?
- Is terminology used consistently throughout the proposal?
- Is the client's name spelled correctly in every instance?

- Are the headings and page numbers correct?
- Are references to other sections, pages, or questions accurate?

Proofreading your own work is good, but not 100 percent reliable. You'll have read your proposal so many times that you may gloss over mistakes. Do a round of editing and proofreading yourself, then find a second (or even third) set of eyes to review it. Once you're sure that it's as perfect as it can be, you'll be confident that it reflects your best work and has you well on the way to winning the deal.

Show attention to detail: Errors in grammar, spelling, and punctuation distract from your message and demonstrate a lapse in the quality and care you're trying to convey to your client.

Make proofreading a priority: No matter how pressed for time you may be, schedule time to make sure your document is comprehensive, consistent, and grammatically correct.

Pass it around: Have a fresh set of eyes review your proposal or presentation to ensure you haven't missed anything and give you confidence that it's as "perfect" as it can be.

"My experience of the world is that things left to themselves don't get right."

—Thomas Henry Huxley, British biologist and educator

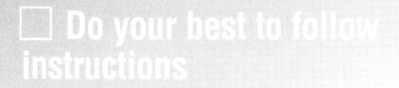

☐ Do your best to follow instructions

☑ *Go to extraordinary lengths to follow instructions*

*P*eople with culinary talents often tell novices, "If you can read, you can cook." Sometimes it's just not that easy. You would think that when it comes to proposals, simply doing what the client asks would be a no-brainer. But surprisingly, one of the main complaints clients have is that the proposals they receive rarely follow their directions.

With that said, you'll have a tremendous advantage over your competition by following directions as if the entire deal depends on it. And sometimes it does. Don't just give it the old college try, go to extraordinary lengths to make sure your proposal follows each and every one of the client's directions, no matter how minor they may seem.

Government organizations, in particular, are notorious for requiring that vendors follow explicit instructions in their proposals. These are often not limited to content; they may also include directions on spacing, page numbering, and even font type and size. As a rule of thumb, you can assume that the more instructions you're given, the more important it is to the client that you follow them exactly.

Start by reading the Request for Proposal (RFP) thoroughly and highlighting key issues and instructions the client has provided. It often helps to make a checklist of items of which you'll need to be aware before, during, and after you write the proposal. You don't want to find out at the end of the process that you were supposed to use letters instead of numbers to delineate your responses and 10.5-point type in a font that you don't even have!

Double-check that your proposal follows every instruction; make this part of the editing and review process. Along with using perfect grammar and appropriate, persuasive content, your ability to follow directions will mean the difference between a "valiant effort" and a winning proposal.

Go in the right direction: One of the most common complaints clients have is that proposals don't follow their directions. Make sure your proposal is the one that does.

Read, learn, do: Make sure that from the very start you've read and understood and are prepared to follow the directions, no matter how negligible they may appear.

Check and double check: As part of your editing and review process, make sure you've followed each and every instruction, to ensure your proposal is decisively poised to win the deal.

"It is no use saying, 'We are doing our best.' You have got to succeed in doing what is necessary."

—Winston Churchill

The McGraw-Hill
Professional Education Series

How to Manage Performance: 24 Lessons for Improving Performance

By Robert Bacal (0-07-143531-X)

Goal-focused, commonsense techniques for stimulating greater productivity in the workplace and fostering true commitment.

Dealing with Difficult People: 24 Lessons for Bringing Out the Best in Everyone

By Rick Brinkman and Rick Kirschner (0-07-141641-2)

Learn about the 10 types of problem people and how to effectively respond to them to improve communication and collaboration.

How to Motivate Every Employee: 24 Proven Tactics to Spark Productivity in the Workplace

By Anne Bruce (0-07-141333-2)

By a master motivator and speaker, this book quickly reviews practical ways you can turn on employees and enhance their performance and your own.

Six Sigma for Managers: 24 Lessons to Understand and Apply Six Sigma Principles in Any Organization

By Greg Brue (0-07-145548-5)

Introduces the fundamental concepts of Six Sigma and details practical steps to spearhead a Six Sigma program in the workplace.

How To Be a Great Coach: 24 Lessons for Turning on the Productivity of Every Employee

By Marshall J. Cook (0-07-143529-8)

Today's most effective coaching methods to dramatically improve the performance of your employees.

Leadership When the Heat's On: 24 Lessons in High Performance Management

By Danny Cox and John Hoover (0-07-141406-1)

Learn hands-on techniques for infusing any company with results-driven leadership at every level, especially during times of organizational turmoil.

Networking for Career Success: 24 Lessons for Getting to Know the Right People

By Diane Darling (0-07-145603-1)

Learn the steps for making mutually beneficial career connections and the know-how to cultivate those connections for the benefit of everyone involved.

Why Customers Don't Do What You Want Them To: 24 Solutions to Common Selling Problems

By Ferdinand Fournies (0-07-141750-8)

This results-focused guidebook will help you to recognize and resolve twenty common selling problems and objections and help you move beyond them.

The Powell Principles: 24 Lessons from Colin Powell, a Legendary Leader

By Oren Harari (0-07-141109-7)

Colin Powell's success as a leader is universally acknowledged. Quickly learn his approach to leadership and the methods he uses to move people and achieve goals.

Project Management: 24 Lessons to Help You Master Any Project

By Gary Heerkens (0-07-145087-4)

An overview for first-time project managers that details what is expected of him or her and how to quickly get the lay of the land.

The Welch Way: 24 Lessons from the World's Greatest CEO

By Jeffrey A. Krames (0-07-138750-1)

Quickly learn some of the winning management practices that made Jack Welch one of the most successful CEOs ever.

The Lombardi Rules: 26 Lessons from Vince Lombardi–the World's Greatest Coach

By Vince Lombardi, Jr. (0-07-141108-9)

A quick course on the rules of leadership behind Coach Vince Lombardi and how anyone can use them to achieve extraordinary results.

Making Teams Work: 24 Lessons for Working Together Successfully

By Michael Maginn (0-07-143530-1)

Guidelines for molding individual team members into a solid, functioning group.

Managing in Times of Change: 24 Tools for Managers, Individuals, and Teams

By Michael Maginn (0-07-144911-6)

Straight talk and actionable advice on making sure that any manager, team, or individual moves through change successfully.

Persuasive Proposals and Presentations: 24 Lessons for Writing Winners

By Heather Pierce (0-07-145089-0)

A short, no-nonsense approach to writing proposals and presentations that sell.

The Sales Success Handbook: 20 Lessons to Open and Close Sales Now

By Linda Richardson (0-07-141636-6)

Learn how the consultative selling approach makes everyone in the transaction a winner. Close more sales and create long-term relationships with customers.

How to Plan and Execute Strategy: 24 Steps to Implement Any Corporate Strategy Successfully

By Wallace Stettinius, D. Robley Wood, Jr., Jacqueline L. Doyle, and John L. Colley, Jr. (0-07-145604-X)

Outlines a field-proven framework to design and implement a corporate strategy that strengthens an organization's competitive advantage.

The New Manager's Handbook: 24 Lessons for Mastering Your New Role

By Morey Stettner (0-07-141334-0)

Here are 24 quick, sensible, and easy-to-implement practices to help new managers succeed from day one.

Finance for Non-Financial Managers: 24 Lessons to Understand and Evaluate Financial Health

> By Katherine Wagner (0-07-145090-4)

> This guide offers a bundle of lessons to clearly explain financial issues in layman's terms.

Getting Organized at Work: 24 Lessons to Set Goals, Establish Priorities, and Manage Your Time

> By Ken Zeigler (0-07-145779-8)

> Supplies tips, tools, ideas, and strategies for becoming more organized with work tasks and priorities in order to get more done in less time.

The Handbook for Leaders: 24 Lessons for Extraordinary Leadership

> By John H. Zenger and Joseph Folkman (0-07-143532-8)

> A workplace-tested prescription for encouraging the behaviors and key drivers of effective leadership, from one of today's top training teams.

Outside the USA, order multiple copies of McGraw-Hill Professional Education titles from:

Asia
McGraw-Hill Education (Asia)
Customer Service Department
60 Tuas Basin Link, Singapore 638775
Tel: (65)6863 1580
Fax: (65) 6862 3354
Email: mghasia@mcgraw-hill.com

Australia & New Zealand
McGraw-Hill Australia Pty Ltd
82 Waterloo Road
North Ryde, NSW 2113, Australia
Tel: +61-2-9900-1800
Fax: +61-2-9878-8881
Email: CService_Sydney@mcgraw-hill.com

Canada
Special Sales Representative, Trade Division
McGraw-Hill Ryerson Limited
300 Water Street
Whitby, Ontario L1N 9B6
Tel: 1-800-565-5758

Europe, Middle East, Africa
McGraw-Hill Professional, EMEA
Shoppenhangers Road, Maidenhead
Berkshire SL6 2QL, United Kingdom
Tel: +44 (0)1628 502 975
Fax: +44 (0)1628 502 167
Email: emma_gibson@mcgraw-hill.com

Other Areas
For other markets outside of the U.S., e-mail Bonnie Chan at
bonnie_chan@mcgraw-hill.com.

Persuasive Proposals and Presentations
Order Form

1–99 copies	_____ copies @ $7.95 per book
100–499 copies	_____ copies @ $7.75 per book
500–999 copies	_____ copies @ $7.50 per book
1,000–2,499 copies	_____ copies @ $7.25 per book
2,500–4,999 copies	_____ copies @ $7.00 per book
5,000–9,999 copies	_____ copies @ $6.50 per book
10,000 or more copies	_____ copies @ $6.00 per book

Name _____

Title _____

Organization _____

Phone (____)_____

Street address _____

City/State (Country) _____ Zip _____

Fax (____)_____

Purchase order number (if applicable) _____

Applicable sales tax, shipping and handling will be added.

☐ VISA   ☐ MasterCard   ☐ American Express

Account number _____ Exp. date ____

Signature _____

Or call 1-800-842-3075
Corporate, Industry, & Government Sale

The McGraw-Hill Companies, Inc.
2 Penn Plaza
New York, NY 10121-2298